Getting Started with Microsoft Visual C++ 5.0

A Companion to C++ How to Program

D1264816

**Deitel & Deitel
Books and Cyber Classrooms**
published by
Prentice Hall

How to Program **Series**
Java How to Program, 2/E
C How to Program, 2/E
C++ How to Program, 2/E
Getting Started with Microsoft Visual J++ 1.1
    A Companion to Java How to Program 2/E
Getting Started with Microsoft Visual C++ 5.0
    A Companion to C++ How to Program 2/E

Multimedia Cyber Classroom **Series**
C & C++ Multimedia Cyber Classroom, 2/E
Java Multimedia Cyber Classroom, 2/E

A Complete Training Course **Series**
A Complete C++ Training Course, 2/E
A Complete Java Training Course, 2/E

For continuing updates on Prentice Hall and Deitel & Associates, Inc. publications visit the Prentice Hall web site

    `http//www.prenhall.com/deitel`

To communicate with the authors, send email to:

    `deitel@deitel.com`

For information on corporate on-site seminars and public seminars offered by Deitel & Associates, Inc. worldwide, visit:

    `http://www.deitel.com`

GETTING STARTED WITH
MICROSOFT VISUAL C++ 5.0

A Companion to C++ How to Program

SECOND EDITION

H. M. Deitel

Deitel & Associates, Inc.

P. J. Deitel

Deitel & Associates, Inc.

PRENTICE HALL, Upper Saddle River, New Jersey 07458

Editor in Chief: *Marcia Horton*
Acquisitions Editor: *Laura Steele*
Production Editor: *Camille Trentacoste*
Cover Art: *Tamara Newnam Cavallo*
Manufacturing Buyer: *Pat Brown*
Multimedia Manager: *Yvette Raven*
Editorial Assistant: *Kate Kaibni*

© 1999 by Prentice-Hall, Inc.
Simon & Schuster / A Viacom Company
Upper Saddle River, New Jersey 07458

Printed in the United States of America

10 9 8 7 6 5 4 3 2 1

ISBN 0-13-082659-6

Prentice-Hall International (UK) Limited, London
Prentice-Hall of Australia Pty. Limited, Sydney
Prentice-Hall Canada Inc., Toronto
Prentice-Hall Hispanoamericana, S.A., Mexico
Prentice-Hall of India Private Limited, New Delhi
Prentice-Hall of Japan, Inc., Tokyo
Simon & Schuster of Asia Pte. Ltd., Singapore
Editora Prentice-Hall do Brasil, Ltda., Rio de Janeiro

Contents

Illustrations

Preface

[Note: Please read the Preface to *C++ How to Program (Second Edition)* before reading this Preface to *Getting Started with Visual C++*.]

Welcome to Visual C++! This appendix is part of a package we designed with Microsoft to help you start creating, editing, and evolving C++ applications in the Microsoft Visual C++ environment. In this package we have provided you with *C++ How to Program (Second Edition)*—The world's leading introductory/intermediate C++ textbook, a CD-ROM, and this appendix—*Getting Started with Visual C++*.

The CD contains *Microsoft's Visual C++ 5.0 Learning Edition* software, code examples from *C++ How to Program (Second Edition)*, and links to many interesting World Wide Web sites that contain extensive C++ resource material. To install *Visual C++* run the **setup.exe** program located on the CD. If you have any problems accessing the code examples on the CD, please download the files directly from our website—

> **www.deitel.com/products_and_services/publications/**
> **index.htm**

The vast majority of programs in *C++ How to Program (Second Edition)* successfully compile with the Microsoft Visual C++ 5.0 compiler. A listing of the few programs that do not compile properly with this compiler, as well as appropriate fixes can be found on our web site at

> **www.deitel.com/products_and_services/publications/**
> **cpp5_0.htm**

We hope you enjoy this package and programming in Visual C++!

A Tour of the Appendix

Section 1—Introduction—discusses how to get started with Visual C++ and the *Microsoft Developer Studio* environment.

Section 2—Microsoft Developer Studio Environment Overview: Visual C++— explains the basics of the integrated development environment for Visual C++—*Microsoft Developer Studio*. This previews a few of the topics that will be covered extensively in the remainder of the section (i.e., the editor, compiler, and debugger).

Section 3—On-line Visual C++ Information—discusses the on-line documentation provided with Visual C++. A thorough explanation of menu items and toolbars provides insight on navigating through the on-line documentation. The on-line documentation is "web-based" and contains a start page. Hyperlinks allow programmers to quickly investigate a specific topic to find answers.

Section 4—Creating and Executing a C++ Application—explains how to create, save, and execute an application in Visual C++. Each procedure is explained in the text and paired with a screen capture illustrating the corresponding menu selections. Helpful environment features of *Microsoft Developer Studio* such as *syntax color highlighting*—the coloring of keywords, comments, and values—are also discussed in this section.

Section 5—Creating a Project in Visual C++—introduces the concept of a *project*— a group of program files associated with an application that resides in a specific directory. All programs compiled in Visual C++ use projects. Subsequent sections discuss projects and project options in more detail.

Section 6—C++ and ActiveX: Using an ActiveX Control in a C++ Program— explains how to create a dialog-based program using the *MFC Application Wizard*. The resource editor is used to edit a dialog box. An ActiveX control is then inserted into the dialog box. Finally, the application is executed. This section offers an introductory discussion of ActiveX controls and COM (Microsoft's Component Object Model).

Section 7—Debugger—helps programmers find code that does not violate the syntax of C++ but may contain logic errors (e.g., infinite loops, division by zero, off-by-one errors, etc.). The debug toolbar and menu contain the tools necessary to debug a C++ application. Capabilities such as watching variable values change as a program executes are discussed.

Section 8—Resources and Demos—is a compilation of some of the most popular sites on the World Wide Web pertaining to ActiveX, C++, COM, and Visual C++.

Acknowledgments

One of the great pleasures of writing a textbook is acknowledging the efforts of the many people whose names may not appear on the cover, but without whose hard work, cooperation, friendship, and understanding producing this appendix would have been impossible.

We are fortunate to have been able to work on this project with a talented and dedicated team of publishing professionals at Prentice Hall. This appendix happened because of the encouragement, enthusiasm, and persistence of our computer science editor, Laura Steele, and her boss, Marcia Horton—Editor-in-Chief of Prentice Hall's Engineering, Science, and Mathematics Division.

Four other people at Deitel & Associates, Inc. devoted long hours to this project. We would like to acknowledge the efforts of Tem Nieto, Chris Poirier, Barbara Deitel and Abbey Deitel.

Our colleagues Tem Nieto and Chris Poirier at Deitel and Associates, Inc.'s Publishing Division contributed long hours of painstaking effort helping us form this special appendix. Tem Nieto, a graduate of the Massachusetts Institute of Technology, is one of our full-time colleagues at Deitel & Associates, Inc. Tem teaches C, C++, Java, and Visual Basic™ seminars and works with us on textbook writing, course development and multimedia authoring efforts.

It is a pleasure to acknowledge the contributions of Mr. Chris Poirier to this work. Chris is a junior at the University of Rhode Island where he majors in Computer Science. He put long hours into developing many of the examples and explanations in this appendix, and he prepared the index. His efforts were crucial to us in meeting the difficult publishing deadlines we faced.

Barbara Deitel researched the quotes. Abbey Deitel researched the Internet and World Wide Web resources. Abbey asks that you send URLs for your favorite Visual C++ sites to her by email at **deitel@deitel.com**

We owe special thanks to the creativity of Tamara Newnam who did the art work for our programming tips icons and the cover. She created the delightful creature who shares with you the book's programming tips.

We owe a great to deal Susanne Peterson of Microsoft who sponsored our efforts and moved mountains to help us form this unique product for you.

We would greatly appreciate your comments, criticisms, corrections, and suggestions for improving the text.

deitel@deitel.com

Harvey M. Deitel
Paul J. Deitel
Sudbury, Massachusetts
June, 1998

About Deitel & Associates, Inc.

Deitel & Associates, Inc. is an internationally recognized corporate training and publishing organization specializing in programming languages, object technology, and technology education. The company provides courses on Java™, C++, C, Visual Basic™, Internet, Smalltalk, Object-Oriented Analysis and Design, COM, DCOM, ActiveX™, CORBA, and many other topics. The principals of Deitel & Associates, Inc. are Dr. Harvey M. Deitel and Paul J. Deitel. The company's clients include some of the world's largest computer companies, government agencies and business organizations. Through its publishing partnership with Prentice Hall, Deitel & Associates, Inc. publishes leading-edge programming textbooks, professional books, interactive CD-ROM based multimedia *Cyber Classrooms, web-based courses,* and satellite courses. Deitel & Associates, Inc. and the authors can be reached via email at `deitel@deitel.com`

To learn more about Deitel & Associates, Inc. and its on-site course curriculum, visit:

`http://www.deitel.com`

To learn more about Deitel & Deitel Prentice Hall publications, visit:

`http://www.prenhall.com/deitel`

For a current list of Deitel/Prentice Hall publications including textbooks and multimedia packages, and for complete worldwide ordering information, please see the last few pages of the textbook that accompanies this package.

E

Getting Started with Microsoft Visual C++

Objectives

- To understand how C++ and Visual C++ relate to each other.
- To use Visual C++ to create, compile and execute C++ programs.
- To understand the Microsoft Developer Studio integrated development environment.
- To use the AppWizard to create C++ Applications.
- To use the debugger to locate program logic errors.
- To be able to integrate C++ and ActiveX.
- To understand visual programming.

If you build it, he will come.
William P. Kinsella

Here Skugg lies snug
As a bug in a rug.
Benjamin Franklin

Change the environment; do not try to change man.
Richard Buckminster Fuller

Outline

E.1 Introduction

Welcome to Visual C++! In this appendix (co-authored with our colleagues, Mr. Tem Nieto and Mr. Chris Poirier of Deitel & Associates, Inc.), you will learn how to create, execute, debug and evolve C++ programs using the powerful C++ development environment from Microsoft—Visual C++. When you complete this appendix, you will be able to use Visual C++ to take full advantage of C++ as you start building substantial applications. As you will see, Visual C++ also enables programmers to take advantage of other powerful Microsoft technologies such as *ActiveX controls*. ActiveX controls are components written in C++, Java or other programming languages that can be "plugged" into a program to provide access to a wide variety of preexisting or user-defined capabilities.

   We have provided *Microsoft Visual C++ 5 Learning Edition* and *Internet Explorer 4* for you on the CD-ROM included in this package. The CD-ROM also contains the 248 applets and applications from *C++ How to Program, Second Edition* in which we explain C++ concepts that apply to all C++ programming environments. This appendix covers the materials specific to C++ programming with Visual C++. The full documentation for the Visual C++ Learning Edition software is included on the CD-ROM. We think you will enjoy programming in C++ with this powerful environment.

E.2 Microsoft Developer Studio Environment Overview: Visual C++

Figure E.1 shows a screen image of the *Microsoft Developer Studio (MDS)*—the integrated development environment that includes Visual C++. This environment contains everything you need to create C++ programs—an *editor* (for typing and correcting your C++ programs), a *compiler* (for translating your C++ programs into machine language code), a *debugger* (for finding logic errors in your C++ programs after they are compiled) and much more. The environment contains many menus and buttons that facilitate editing, compiling and debugging your C++ applications. We discuss the features associated with many of these menus and buttons in subsequent sections.

Back   Forward   Stop   Refresh   Home   Search

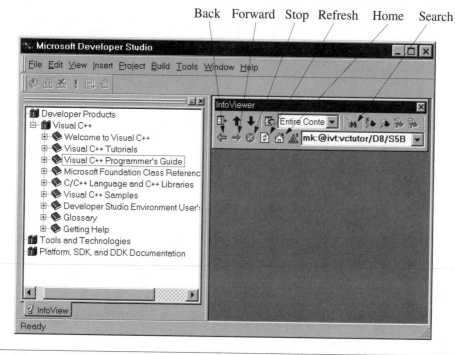

Fig. E.1   Microsoft Developer Studio (Visual C++).

E.3 On-line Visual C++ Information

Developer Studio provides on-line documentation for C++ and Visual C++ in the **Info-View** *pane (Fig. E.1)*. Information about all aspects of Visual C++ is available—from the Standard C++ Library supplied with most recent C++ compilers to the Microsoft Foundation Classes (MFC) used for programming Windows applications. Topics are displayed in *tree-view format*. Click the left mouse button on the plus (+) sign next to a topic to expand the topic's subcategories (Fig. E.2). Note: For the rest of this appendix, we refer to *"clicking the left mouse button"* simply as *clicking*. Notice the enlarged **InfoView** pane. The **InfoView** pane is resized by dragging the resize bars at its bottom edge or its right edge.

Notice in Figure E.1 the **Infoviewer** toolbar. The toolbar is used to navigate through on-line documentation in a similar manner to viewing pages in a web browser. The left and right arrows go back and forward, respectively, through the pages viewed previously. The **Stop** button causes the program to stop loading the current topic. The **Refresh** button reloads the current topic from the document's source. The toolbar also provides a **Home** button that displays the **InfoViewer** page, the home page for on-line documentation. The **Search** button allows a programmer to search throughout the entire contents of the on-line documentation.

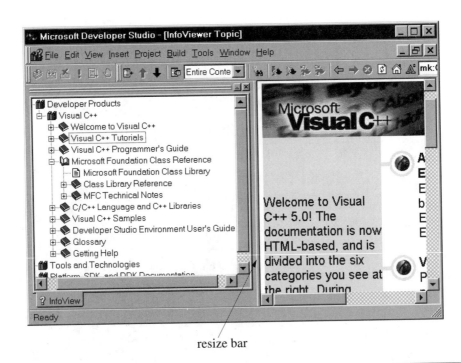

Fig. E.2   Resized **InfoView** window with subcategories.

On-line information is divided into categories. Each category is preceded by a book icon. The **Welcome to Visual C++** category introduces the programmer to the **Visual C++ Start Page**—the starting point for an HTML-based approach to the on-line documentation. The **What's New** item explains the newest features introduced in Visual C++ version 5.0. The **Enterprise Edition**, **Professional Edition** and **Learning Edition** sections describe the different features in each edition of Visual C++.

The **Visual C++ Tutorials** category helps programmers learn how to develop applications in Visual C++. The tutorials contain more advanced issues such as developing OLE server applications, creating OLE containers and creating ActiveX controls.

The **Visual C++ Programmer's Guide** category contains information illustrating how to create your first program, compile a program, create user interfaces and debug programs. The programmers guide also provides a quick reference for C++ keywords and operators.

The **Microsoft Foundation Class Reference** category provides a complete reference to the variables, functions and classes associated with the Microsoft Foundation Classes (MFC). The category also includes sample programs, MFC technical notes, a hierarchy chart and a class library reference.

The **C/C++ Language and C++ Libraries** category contains information about the Active Template Library (ATL)—A set of C++ class templates that make programming with COM easier and complete references to the C++ language, the C language and the standard C++ libraries.

The *Visual C++ Samples* category provides sub-categories with example programs for some of the newest features in Visual C++. Sample programs are included for the Active Template Library (ATL), AppWizards and MFC.

The *User's Guide* category contains information about working with projects, working with editors and customizing the look and feel of the Developer Studio environment (such as windows, toolbars, keyboard shortcuts to commands and adding customized tools to the *Tools* menu). The **User's Guide** also provides references for several utility programs that come with Visual C++.

The *Developer Studio Environment Guide* category contains information on the new features of Developer Studio, working with classes, working with projects, wizards, resource editors and windows utilities.

The *Glossary* contains a listing of terminology for the Developer Studio, copyright information for Visual C++ and accessibility information for people with disabilities.

Finally, the *Getting Help* category provides information on how to get help in the Developer Studio environment and a frequently asked questions sub-category.

E.4 Creating and Executing a C++ Application

This section demonstrates how to create and execute a C++ application. The first step in writing an application is to create a new C++ source file. Select *New...* from the *File menu*. This will open the *New dialog*. Click the **Files** tab and notice the different types of files that appear. Select *C++ Source File* and click the **OK** button. Notice that a new window appears entitled **Cpp1** (Fig E.3). Usage of other file formats will be discussed later in this appendix.

Fig. E.3 Displaying a code window (**Cpp1**).

The next step is to type the C++ code into the **Cpp1** window. Click anywhere in the **Cpp1** window to begin typing. For the purposes of this example, type the program of Fig. 1.4 from *C++ How to Program, Second Edition*. Once you begin typing notice that an asterisk (*****) appears to the right of **Cpp1**. The asterisk indicates that the file has been modified and should be saved. Once the file is saved, the asterisk will disappear. To save the program, select **Save** from the **File** menu as shown in Fig. E.4.

Although you selected **Save**, the **Save As** *dialog* appears (Fig. E.5). The first time a file is saved, the **Save As** dialog is displayed. Use this dialog to specify the file name and the directory in which to save the file. Type the file's name (**Welcome.cpp**) into the **File name** field. You can specify the file's directory in the **Save in** drop-down list. We created the directory **C++ Programs** to store our program—you may specify any directory you wish. After you specify the directory and file name, click the **Save** *button*.

When the file is saved, the title of the window containing the program changes from **Cpp1** to the file name **Welcome.cpp**. Any file name with the extension **cpp** is officially recognized by Developer Studio as a C++ source file.

Developer Studio imposes a coloring scheme (called syntax color highlighting) on the program elements in a C++ source file—you might have noticed this while you were typing your first program. Syntax color highlighting is applied as you type your code and is applied to all C++ files opened in Developer Studio.

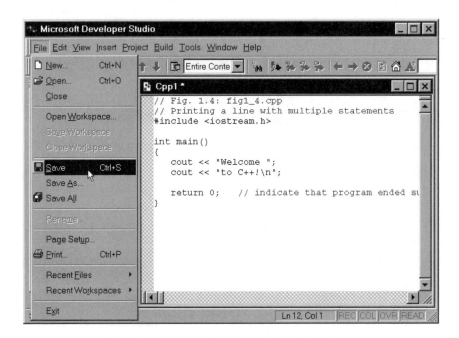

Fig. E.4   Selecting **Save** from the **File** menu.

Fig. E.5   Save As dialog.

In Fig. E.6, notice that the comment at the beginning of the program (green on the screen) and some of the C++ keywords (blue on the screen) are a lighter color. The colors help the user differentiate between keywords, comments and other text. Keywords normally appear in blue, comments in green and other text in black, but you can set your own color preferences.

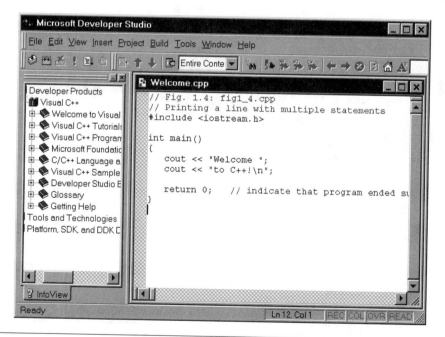

Fig. E.6   Saved source file with syntax color highlighting.

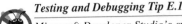

Testing and Debugging Tip E.1

Microsoft Developer Studio's syntax color highlighting helps the programmer avoid using keywords accidentally as variable names.

To customize the syntax color highlighting, select the **Options...** item from the **Tools** menu. In the **Options** *dialog*, click the right arrow in the upper-right corner of the dialog until the **Format** *tab* appears and click the **Format** tab. All syntax coloring aspects of the entire Developer Studio can be customized here. To change the syntax coloring for your C++ source code, select **Source Windows** from the **Category** box in the upper-left corner of the dialog. In the right side of the dialog, the **Font, Size, Foreground** and **Background** areas enable you to customize each language element. Simply click the element in the **Colors** area, then use the **Font, Size, Foreground** and **Background** areas to customize the language element. Click **OK** when you have finished customizing.

The program is now ready to be compiled. From the **Build** menu select **Compile Welcome.cpp** as seen in (Fig. E.7) to begin the compilation process (i.e., the translation process). *Note:* The **Compile** option is disabled unless a C++ *source file* window has the focus. A window with the focus is the active window and is indicated by a darker title bar (where the window's title is displayed) than other windows. You can click a window to activate it and give it the focus. When the **Compile** option is selected, the dialog shown in Fig. E.8 appears.

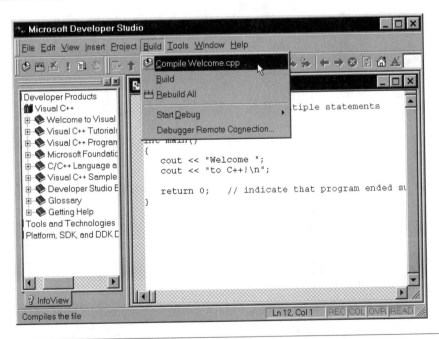

Fig. E.7   Selecting **Compile** from the **Build** menu.

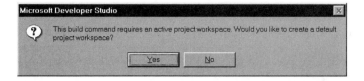

Fig. E.8   Dialog Displayed when the **Compile** option is selected.

Compiling a program requires a project. A *project* is a group of C++ files stored in a directory. Projects enable the programmer to manage as one unit all the files required for a particular application. The user does not explicitly have to create a project because Developer Studio gives the user the option of using a *default project*. For this example we use the default project. Click **Yes** to create a default project and compile the project's C++ source files. The default project is a *Console Application* (in subsequent sections we discuss projects in more detail). Figure E.9 shows the environment after a successful compilation.

Any compiler errors or compiler warnings appear in the ***Output*** window (Fig. E.9) at the bottom of Developer Studio. A *compiler error* indicates that code in the program violates the syntax (i.e., the grammatical rules) of C++ (also known as a *syntax error*). A program cannot execute if it contains compiler errors—the errors must first be corrected and the program must be recompiled. A *compiler warning* indicates that a statement is syntactically correct but may cause a problem at run time. Compiler warnings are not as severe as compiler errors—programs with warnings normally can execute.

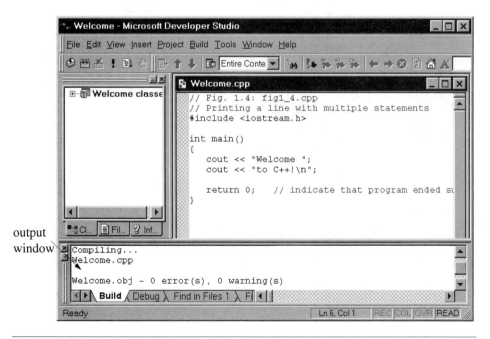

Fig. E.9   Environment after compilation.

Testing and Debugging Tip E.2

If your program contains compiler errors, double click on an error message in the output window to locate the offending line of code. Visual C++ places a blue arrow next to the line of code in the source file.

Once the C++ source file has been successfully compiled (no compiler errors), the object code for the program is stored in an object file called **Welcome.obj**. Before the program can be executed, the console application must be "built"—the object code is *linked* with libraries defined elsewhere that will allow the application to execute on a computer running the Windows operating system. Refer to Section 1.12 of *C++ How to Program* for more information concerning the linking process. To start the build process select **Build Welcome.exe** from the **Build** menu as seen in Fig E.10. *Note:* The **Build** option will compile a C++ source file if the program is not already compiled.

The program is now ready for execution. Select **Execute Welcome.exe** from the **Build** menu (Fig. E.11). When the program executes a console window is displayed (i.e. a DOS window). All program input and output occurs in this window. A screen capture of **Welcome.exe** running in a console window appears in Fig. E.12.

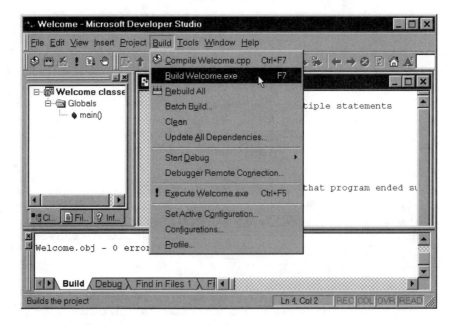

Fig. E.10 Selecting the **Build Welcome.exe** item from the **Build** menu.

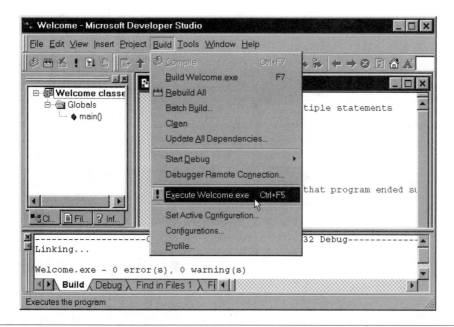

Fig. E.11 Selecting **Execute Welcome.exe** from the **Build** menu.

Fig. E.12 **Welcome.exe** running in a console window.

E.5 Creating a Project in Visual C++

Visual C++ allows programmers to manage application development with *projects*. Projects organize code and allow a programmer to easily manipulate many different types of program related files. In this section, we create a project, add a simple application to it and execute the application. For demonstration purposes, we use the program of Fig. 2.24 in *C++ How to Program*. [*Note:* Before you begin the new application in this section, close the previous project by selecting **Close Workspace** from the **File** menu. A dialog box appears asking, **"Do you want to close all document windows?"** Click **Yes**. Repeat this process each time you are ready to begin a new program.]

To create a project for an application, first select **New...** from the **File** menu to display the **New** dialog (Fig. E.13). Click the **Projects** *tab* and highlight **Win32 Console Application**. Select the directory in which the program should be stored by clicking the

... button to the right of the **_Location_** field. Name the project **ProjectExample**. Notice that the name of the project is added to the directory path in the **Location** field. Each project is normally stored in its own directory. Click the **OK** button to create the project. Note that the **OK** button is disabled unless a name is specified in the **_Project Name_** field.

Next, create a new **C++ Source File** to display a *source window* in which to type your program. Save the file as **ProjectExample.cpp** by selecting **Save** from the **File** menu. The **_Save As_** dialog appears (Fig. E.14). Enter the name **ProjectExample.cpp** in the **File name** field and click the **Save** button.

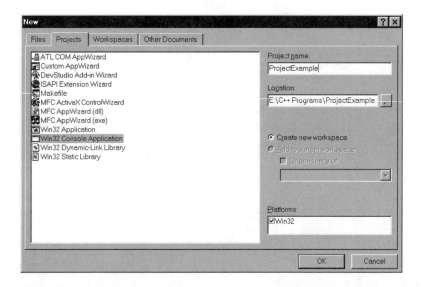

Fig. E.13 **Projects** tab of the **New** dialog.

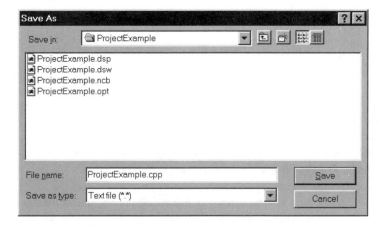

Fig. E.14 **Save As** dialog.

Now type the program of Fig. 2.24. Note that as the C++ code is typed, the environment imposes syntax coloring highlighting. Figure E.15 shows the environment with the program in the source window.

The program file is not currently part of the project. Therefore, it must be added to the project so it can be compiled and executed. Select **Add To Project** from the **Project** menu and click on **Files**. This will open the **Insert Files into Project** dialog (Fig. E.16). Select the file **ProjectExample.cpp** and click the **OK** button. Note: If a project consists of multiple source files, each file must be inserted into the project using the **Insert Files into Project** dialog. The *Shift* and *Ctrl* keys can be used to select multiple files at once for insertion.

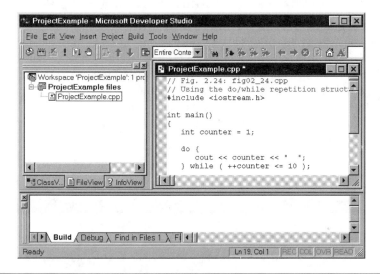

Fig. E.15 Developer Studio environment after the application is entered.

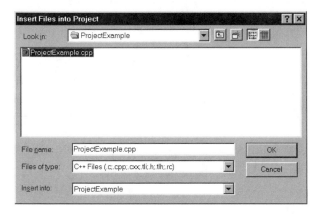

Fig. E.16 Insert Files into Project dialog.

The project is now ready to be compiled. Click the **Build** button on the toolbar (Fig. E.17) to *build* (i.e. compile) a project. Building a project recompiles all C++ source files changed since the last build operation. The **Build** tab in the **Output** window at the bottom of MDS displays the result of the build.

The application executes in a console window (Fig. E.18). The console is a DOS window that displays the program output and allows the user to input data required by the program. When the application terminates, press any key to return to the Developer Studio environment.

E.6 C++ and ActiveX: Using an ActiveX Control in a C++ Program

Visual C++ enables programmers to create and use *ActiveX controls*. ActiveX controls are reusable components written in Visual C++, Java, Visual Basic, or other languages that can be "plugged" into a program written in Visual C++. An ActiveX control can be just about anything the programmer can imagine—a calendar, a word processor, an image editor, a card game, etc. ActiveX controls can be visible or invisible to the user of the application. For example, a card game ActiveX control would certainly be visible to allow the user to play the game and an ActiveX control that performs a sorting algorithm would be invisible to the user.

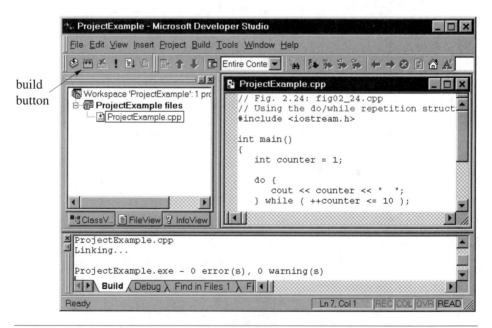

Fig. E.17 Environment after a successful build.

Fig. E.18 Console window containing `ProjectExample.exe`.

ActiveX controls are the natural evolution of *Object Linking and Embedding (OLE) controls*. OLE controls allowed *in-place activation* (also called *visual editing*) where the OLE control acted as a host container for another control. For example, a Microsoft Word document could act as an OLE container and host a Microsoft Excel spreadsheet. This capability allowed the Word user to edit an Excel spreadsheet without ever opening Excel or leaving Word. ActiveX controls improve upon OLE controls by providing distributed capabilities for applications executing on multiple computers over a network and by providing a more efficient design.

ActiveX controls are built using Microsoft's *Component Object Model (COM)*. COM is a *binary level specification* that describes a procedure by which objects communicate. The complete specification can be viewed at

`http://www.microsoft.com/com`

At the heart of the COM specification is a software architecture that stresses reuse. The COM specification outlines a system based upon reusable *components* (software pieces that exist in binary form).

Components written in one language can interact with components written in a completely different language. The interaction is accomplished through COM which is language independent, location independent and compiler independent.

 Portability Tip E.1

COM is language independent, compiler independent and location independent.

COM components fall into one of three categories *in-process servers*, *local servers* or *remote servers*. In-process server components are implemented as code libraries loaded *dynamically* (i.e., at run-time) by the operating system. These code libraries are called *dynamic link libraries (DLLs)*. DLLs are always loaded into the same memory address space as the calling process and are therefore not complete stand-alone applications. ActiveX controls are in-process server components.

A local server component runs as a separate executable on the same machine. An example of a local server is Internet Explorer. A remote server component runs as a separate executable on a remote machine (connected to via a network). Communication is accomplished through *Distributed COM (DCOM)*. Communication is accomplished through the same COM mechanism—with DCOM performing the distributed communication transparently to the user.

In this section, you need not know all the specifics of COM or DCOM to use ActiveX controls. We discuss the integration of an ActiveX control into a Visual C++ program. We outline each step of the process.

ActiveX controls can only be placed inside a program that uses the *Microsoft Foundation Classes (MFC)*. MFC is the set of classes that provide the building blocks for Windows applications written in C++. These classes contain implementations of buttons, text fields, dialog boxes, scrollbars, etc. Writing a program that uses *MFC* can be a long and complex process without the help of *AppWizards*. Visual C++ provides programmers the option of using AppWizards—applications that allow programmers to develop the foundation of a Windows application quickly and efficiently. AppWizards helps the programmer by creating a skeleton of the program and implementing basic functionality. The generated code can then be viewed and edited by the programmer to customize the application. The **MFC AppWizard** is a specific AppWizard that allows users to create MFC-based applications quickly. Among its many capabilities, the **MFC AppWizard** allows programmers to specify options for the program type to create, the layout of the application and whether or not comments should be included in the generated code. *Note:* MFC event handling is beyond the scope of this book and appendix. For more information on MFC event handling, see the on-line documentation.

To start the **MFC AppWizard** in Developer Studio select **New...** from the **File** menu. The **New** dialog appears as shown in Fig. E.19. Click the **Projects** tab and select **MFC AppWizard (EXE).** Notice the other **AppWizards** that are available.

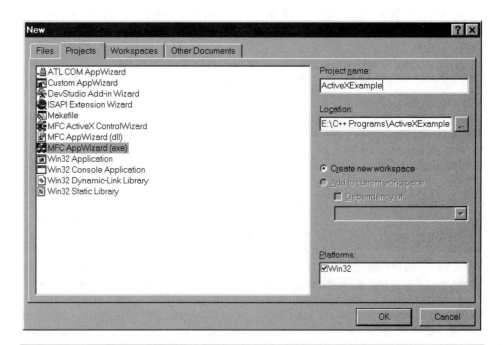

Fig. E.19 Selecting the **MFC AppWizard** from the **New** dialog.

In the **Project Name** field type `ActiveXExample`. Notice that the **Location** field changes accordingly. Click **OK** to start the **MFC AppWizard**.

A new dialog appears titled *MFC AppWizard - Step 1* as seen in Fig E.20. This step allows the programmer to indicate what type of program the **MFC AppWizard** will generate. The **Single Document** creates an application with one document window (also know as a *single document interface* or *SDI* application). The Windows Notepad application is an example of an SDI program. This type of application involves less programming than a *multiple document interface (MDI)*—specified with the *Multiple documents* option. MDI programs allow multiple windows to be opened at the same time in the application. Visual C++ is an example of a multiple document interface. Notice how the image to the left of the radio buttons changes to represent the radio button that is selected. In this example we will not be using either of the two preceding applications. We will, rather, create a *Dialog based* application. **Dialog based** applications replace the main window with a dialog box. All interaction with a user is performed in the dialog. An example of a **Dialog based** application is the Windows Calculator application. Select the **Dialog based** radio button and click **Next >.**

In step two, shown in Fig. E.21, of the **MFC Application Wizard** the **About box, 3D controls** and **ActiveX controls** checkboxes should be selected. Note: If the **ActiveX Controls** checkbox is not selected, this example will not work correctly. The **Title** field contains the words that are displayed in the title bar of the application. By default the title bar is the program name. However, the programmer may change this to better describe the program. Click the **Next >** button to continue.

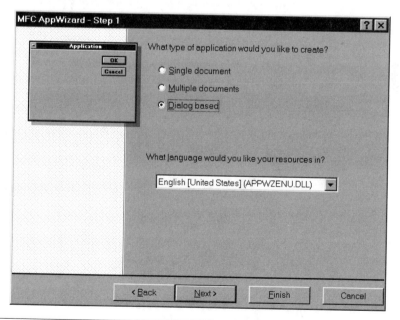

Fig. E.20 **MFC AppWizard - Step 1** dialog.

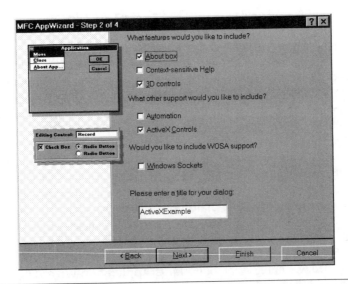

Fig. E.21   MFC AppWizard - Step 2 of 4 dialog.

In step three of the **MFC Application Wizard** select **Yes, Please** as shown in Fig E.22. Comments will be inserted into the program and help the programmer understand what the automatically generated code does and where the programmer needs to add code. The other option specifies how the MFC libraries should be used in the program. For this example we will be using the default, ***As a shared DLL***. Click the **Next >** button to proceed.

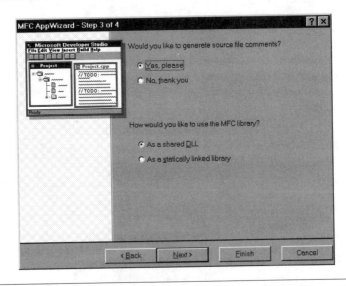

Fig. E.22   MFC APPWizard - Step 3 of 4 dialog.

In the final step of the **MFC AppWizard**, shown in Fig. E.23, a listing of classes appears. These classes will be created by the **MFC AppWizard**. Notice in Fig. E.23 that the dialog displays the **Classname, Header File** and **Implementation File**. Click **Finish** to dismiss the dialog.

When the final step is complete, the **New Project Information** dialog appears (Fig E.24). This dialog displays important information pertaining to the new classes that will be created. For our example the dialog lists the type of program, the classes, the features of the program and the location where the files reside on the hard disk. Dismiss the dialog by clicking **OK**. The **MFC AppWizard** now generates the application. The **MFC App-Wizard** is complete when control returns to the Developer Studio environment.

Before adding an ActiveX control to the program, the programmer must know how to use the ActiveX control. We created an ActiveX control named **deitelshapes.ocx** for you to use in this example. This file must be copied from the CD ROM to your hard drive. This OCX is not known to the operating system yet, so it is considered an *unregistered OCX*.

The **deitelshapes.ocx** file is *registered* using the **regsvr32** program. This program is located in the **c:\windows\system** directory and is available on all Win32 platforms (Note: Your **c:\windows** directory may be named differently. If so, replace **c:\windows** with the appropriate directory name). Figure E.25 shows the **deitelshapes.ocx** file being registered and Fig. E.26 shows the dialog displayed when the OCX is successfully registered. Note: We copied the file **deitelshapes.ocx** into the directory **e:\C++Programs\ActiveXExample** on our system (you may choose to name your directory differently).

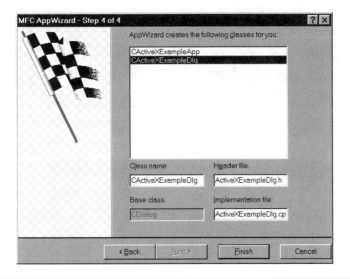

Fig. E.23 MFC AppWizard - Step 4 of 4 dialog.

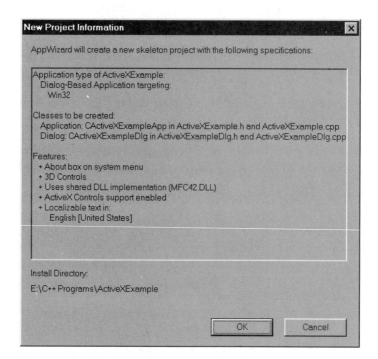

Fig. E.24 New Project Information dialog.

Fig. E.25 Registering the **deitelshapes.ocx** file.

Fig. E.26 Dialog displayed when the **deitelshapes.ocx** file is registered.

Once the OCX is registered, information about that ActiveX control can be viewed by the programmer. Select **OLE/COM Object Viewer** from the **Tools** menu to display the **OLE/COM Object Viewer** program (Fig. E.27). Information about other ActiveX controls and COM objects can be viewed in this application. A small icon indicates the object type. The two primary object types are ActiveX controls and *type libraries*. The `deitelshapes` control is an example of an ActiveX control. If the `deitelshapes.ocx` file is unregistered, the `deitelshapes` control will not be listed. Note that items listed in the **OLE/COM Object Viewer** program may be different on your system. Some of the items shown are from other products that are not necessarily on your system. Select **Exit** from the **File** menu to close the program and return control to Developer Studio.

Most ActiveX controls are designed to handle all of the events that occur within them. We will, therefore, not have to concern ourselves with MFC event handling in this example.

Notice the four different tabs that appear in the **Workspace** pane as seen in Fig E.28. Click the **ResourceView** tab and open the **dialog** folder. Double-click the option labeled **IDD_ACTIVEXEXAMPLE_DIALOG** to bring up the *Resource Editor*. The Resource Editor allows a programmer to quickly assemble a Graphical User Interface (GUI) by adding components to the dialog box. Notice that two buttons and a label appear in the dialog box. These are the default components placed in the program by the **MFC App-Wizard**. Click the **Cancel** button to highlight it and make it active. Press the *Delete* key to remove the button from the dialog box. Now select the label that reads **TODO: Place Dialog Controls Here** and remove it from the dialog as well. The **OK** button will allow the user to exit the program—the default implementation of the button.

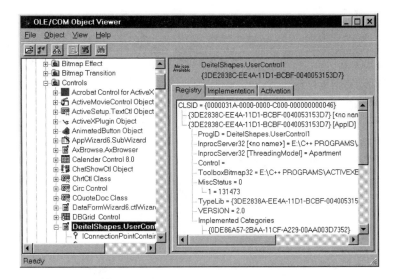

Fig. E.27 OLE/COM Object Viewer showing the `DeitelShapes` ActiveX control.

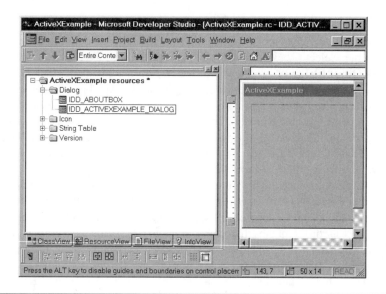

Fig. E.28   Editing a dialog box from the Resource Editor.

We are now ready to place the ActiveX control into the dialog. Place the mouse pointer in a blank area of the dialog and click the right mouse button. A pop up menu will appear. Select the *Insert ActiveX Control* option as seen in Fig E.29.

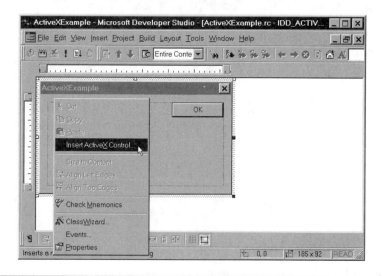

Fig. E.29   Inserting an ActiveX control into a dialog.

The ActiveX control will appear in the dialog (Fig E.30). Resize the ActiveX control to fit into the dialog by clicking and dragging its edges. The **deitelshapes.ocx** ActiveX control can be stretched to any size. When the scroll bar is visible this is a good indication that you have obtained an acceptable height for the control.

When you are finished positioning the components, execute the program. The program will launch in its own window (Fig. E.31).

The **Deitelshapes.ocx** file is a simple ActiveX control that draws shapes. The scrollbar is part of the ActiveX control and changes the shape drawn. Clicking any area of the ActiveX control will start the drawing process. To exit the program click **OK**. The **OK** button is part of the dialog box (Fig E.29) and is not part of the ActiveX control.

E.7 Debugger

MDS contains a built-in debugger. The debugger is useful for finding logic errors in programs. The debugger is not used for syntax checking—that is the job of the compiler. A program must compile successfully before the debugger can be used. The debugger is most commonly used to step through the lines of code on a line-by-line basis, set variable watches to view the values of individual variables at execution time and set *breakpoints* (lines of code selected by the programmer at which execution is halted so the programmer can examine the code and the current state—such as variable values—of the program's execution).

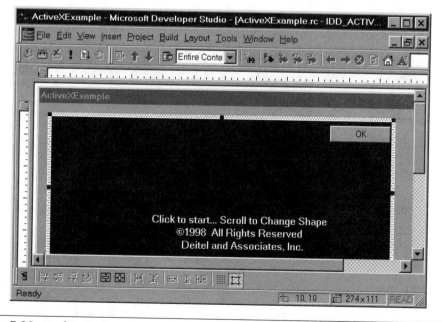

Fig. E.30 Deitelshapes.ocx ActiveX control inserted into dialog.

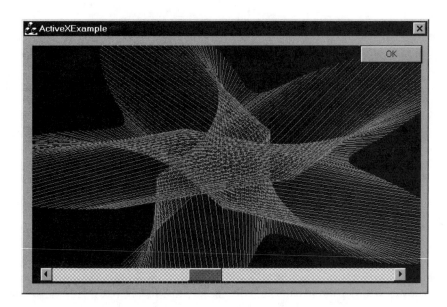

Fig. E.31 ActiveXExample application running in its own window.

A debugging session is started by selecting the **Build** menu's *Start Debug* submenu (Fig. E.32) and selecting *Go.*

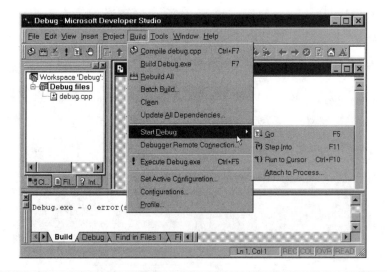

Fig. E.32 Build menu's **Start Debug** submenu.

Breakpoints are used in areas where the programmer wants to examine program execution in more detail. A program can have multiple breakpoints. Breakpoints are set by clicking the line in the program where the breakpoint is desired and clicking the ***Insert/ Remove Breakpoint*** button (Fig. E.33). When a breakpoint is set, a small red dot appears to the left of the line. To set the breakpoint, the cursor must be in the window containing the C++ code; otherwise, the **Insert/Remove Breakpoint** button is grayed. An individual breakpoint can be removed by clicking the line with the breakpoint and clicking **Insert/Remove Breakpoint** on the **Build** minibar. The **Build** minibar and a breakpoint are illustrated in Fig. E.33.

Selecting the **Go** menu item or clicking **Go** on the **Build** minibar (Fig. E.33) starts the debugger. Since we have chosen to debug a console application the console window containing our application appears (Fig. E.34). All program interaction (input and output) is performed in this window. Program execution halts for input and at breakpoints.

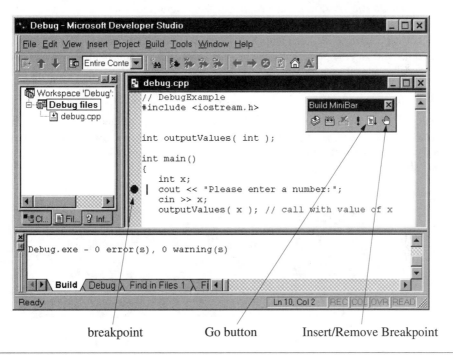

breakpoint   Go button   Insert/Remove Breakpoint

Fig. E.33 Build minibar and a breakpoint.

Fig. E.34 Console Window containing our **Debug** program.

Figure E.35 shows the execution being halted by a breakpoint. Notice the yellow arrow to the left of the statement

```
cout << "Please enter a number:";
```

This arrow indicates the next line of code to be executed. The bottom portion of the window is divided into two parts— the *Variables* window on the left side with three tabs and the *Watch* window on the right side. Note that the **Debug** menu has replaced the **Build** menu in Developer Studio.

Testing and Debugging Tip E.3

*Loops that iterate many times can be skipped by placing a breakpoint after the loop and clicking the **Go** button.*

The **Variables** window contains a list of the program's variables. Note that different variables can be viewed at different times, by clicking either the *Auto, Local* or *this* tabs. The **Auto** tab displays the name and value of the variables or objects used in both the previous statement and the current statement. The **Locals** tab displays the name and current value for all the local variables or objects in the current function's scope. The **this** tab displays data for the object to which the currently executing function belongs.

The variable names listed in the **Variables** window cannot be modified by the user. Often certain variables are monitored by the programmer during the debugging process— a process known as setting a watch. The **Watch** window allows the user to watch variables. When the value of a particular variable changes, the user can immediately see the new value in the **Watch** window.

next line to
execute

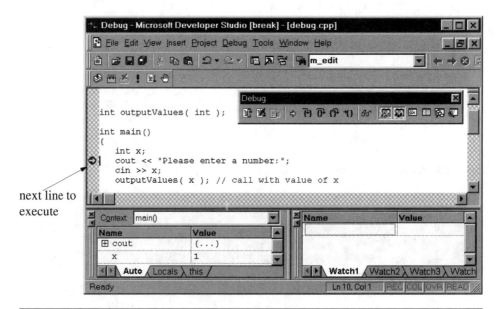

Fig. E.35 The **Variables** window and **Watch** window.

Variables can be typed directly into the **Watch** window or dragged from the **Variables** window and dropped into the **Watch** window. A variable can be deleted from the **Watch** window by highlighting the variable name and pressing the *Delete* key. Watch variables can be grouped by the programmer using the **Watch** window's tabs. Figure E.36 shows a watch set for the variable **x**.

The **Debug** toolbar contains buttons that facilitate the debugging process. These buttons perform the same actions as the **Debug** menu items. Each button is labeled in Fig. E.37. Note: The **Debug** toolbar can be displayed positioning the mouse pointer over any toolbar, clicking the right mouse button and selecting the **Debug** option in the popup menu.

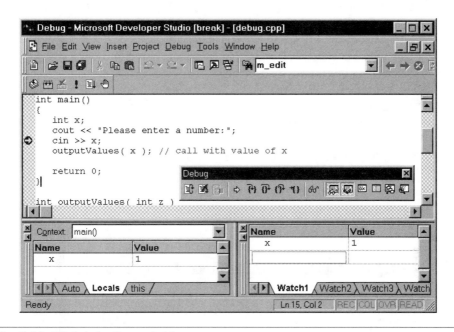

Fig. E.36 Watch for the variable **x**.

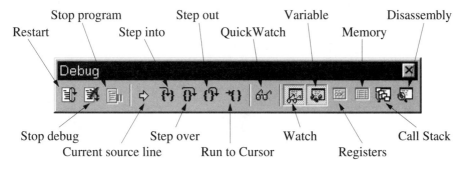

Fig. E.37 Debug toolbar buttons.

The value of a watch variable can be changed by the programmer for testing purposes. Click in the area displaying the current value in the **Watch** window and type a new value. The new value appears in red to indicate that the value has changed since the program last stopped at a breakpoint.

The **Restart** button restarts the program. Control stops at the first breakpoint or executable line requiring input. The **Stop Debugging** button ends the debugging session.

The **Step Over** button executes the next executable line of code and advances the yellow arrow to the next executable line (Fig. E.36) in the program. If the line of code contains a function call, the function is not entered (stepped into), rather it is executed in its entirety. This process allows the user to execute the program on a line-by-line basis and follow the execution of the program.

The **Step Into** button allows functions to be stepped into—such that the user can confirm the proper execution of the function line-by-line. Note: The yellow arrow must point to a line of code containing a function call. The results of the "step into" operation are shown in Fig. E.38. Functions that can be stepped into include programmer-defined functions and C++ library functions.

The **Step Out** button allows the user to step out of the current function and return control back to the line of the function call. Click the **Run to Cursor** button to execute all code up to the line where the cursor is sitting.

Testing and Debugging Tip E.4

The debugger allows the user to "step into" C++ library functions.

Testing and Debugging Tip E.5

*Loops that iterate many times can be skipped by placing the cursor after the loop and clicking the **Run to Cursor** button.*

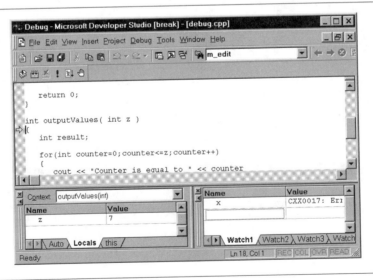

Fig. E.38 Stepping into a function.

The **QuickWatch** button displays the **QuickWatch** *dialog* (Fig. E.39) that is useful for monitoring expressions and variable values. The **QuickWatch** dialog is used to get a "snap shot" of one or more variable values at a point in time during the program's execution. To watch a variable enter the variable name or expression into the **Expression** field and press *Enter*. Note that the **Recalculate** button can be clicked instead of pressing *Enter*. If the programmer wants to maintain a longer watch, the **Add Watch** button can be clicked to add the variable to the **Watch** window. Once the **QuickWatch** dialog is dismissed, variables in the dialog are not preserved. The next time the **QuickWatch** dialog is displayed, both the **name** and **value** fields are empty.

The **Variable** button displays the **Variable** window. The **Watch** button displays the **Watch** window.

The **Call Stack** button displays a window containing the program's *function call stack*. A function call stack is a list of the functions that were called to get to the current line in the program.

The **Disassembly** button displays the disassembled program code. Analyzing a program that has been disassembled is a complex process and is likely to be used by only the most advanced users of Visual C++. We do not discuss the **Disassembly** button in this appendix.

If you close a project and reopen it, the breakpoints set during the debugging session are still there. Breakpoints are persistent. You can gather information about breakpoints by accessing the **Edit** menu's **Breakpoints** menu item. When selected, the **Breakpoints** menu item displays the **Breakpoints** dialog (Fig. E.40).

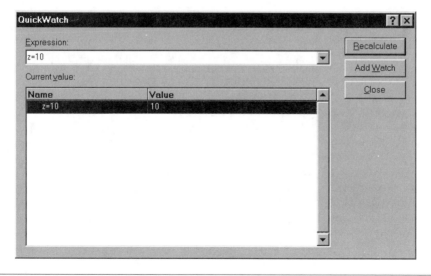

Fig. E.39 QuickWatch dialog.

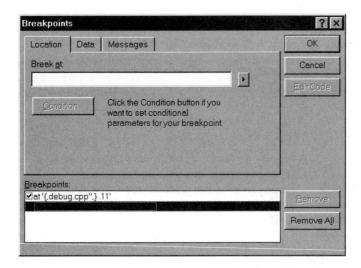

Fig. E.40 Breakpoints dialog.

The **Breakpoints** dialog displays all the breakpoints currently set for the program. A checkbox appears next to each breakpoint. If the breakpoint is active, the checkbox contains a check. If the breakpoint is disabled, the checkbox is empty. Clicking the checkbox allows the user to toggle the breakpoint. Additional breakpoints can be added by entering the desired line number into the ***Break at*** field. Figure E.41 shows a new break point set for line 10. To specify an exact line number for a breakpoint, type the number preceded by a period in the ***Break at*** field.

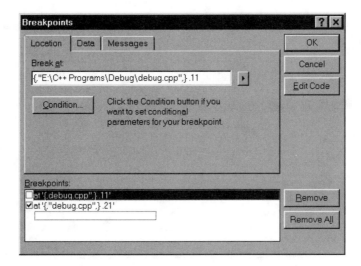

Fig. E.41 Breakpoints dialog with a disabled breakpoint.

Figure E.42 shows the debugging environment with a disabled breakpoint. Notice that the disabled breakpoint is still visible but it appears as a hollow dot. To make the breakpoint active, click the empty checkbox next to the breakpoint in the **Breakpoints** dialog.

Testing and Debugging Tip E.6

Disabled breakpoints allow the programmer to maintain breakpoints in key locations in the program so they can be used again when they are needed. Disabled breakpoints are always visible.

Testing and Debugging Tip E.7

When using the debugger, placing the mouse pointer over a variable name displays the variable's value.

Testing and Debugging Tip E.8

*When using the debugger to trace through a program, certain problems such as infinite loops can arise. These problems can usually be interrupted by selecting **Break** from the **Debug** menu.*

When you have finished your debugging session, click the ***Stop Debugging*** button on the **Debug** toolbar. The environment changes back to the pre-debugging setup. You should refer to the on-line documentation for more details on using the debugger.

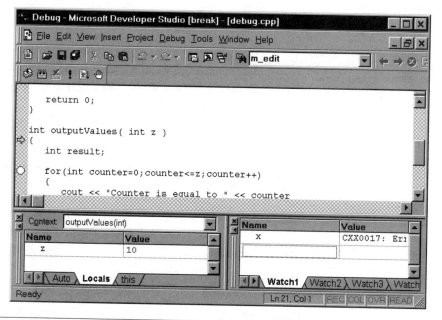

Fig. E.42 Debugging environment with a disabled breakpoint.

E.8   Resources and Demos

[Note: This section was written by Abbey Deitel, a recent graduate of the Industrial Management program at Carnegie Mellon University.] There is a bounty of C++ information on the World Wide Web. Many people are programming in C++ and sharing their thoughts, discoveries, ideas and source code with each other via the Internet. If you would like to recommend other sites, please send us email at

> `deitel@deitel.com`

and we will put links to the sites you suggest on our Web site

> `http://www.prenhall.com/deitel`

The following World Wide Web sites provide information regarding Visual C++, ActiveX, other Microsoft technologies and development tools and C++.

`http://www.microsoft.com/visualc/`

The best place to begin searching for Visual C++ information is the site where the platform was developed. Microsoft's Visual C++ site is one of the most comprehensive sites I have found on Visual C++. You can learn more about Visual C++, check out some great links, find useful product and technical information in the *Technical Materials* section, or get help from Microsoft on-line. The following is a walk-through of the Microsoft Visual C++ site.

The *Start Page* provides headlines containing the most recent news from Microsoft including the latest Visual C++ related products and events.

The *Product Information* option provides an introduction to Visual C++. Links to Product Documentation, Press Articles and an Evaluators guide are also available.

The *Resources* option has links to development strategies and scenarios, user groups, events and seminars and books and magazines.

The *Free Downloads* page offers technology preview software, trial editions and software patches.

`http://www.pinpub.com/vcd/home.htm`

Visit this site if you want to read an issue of Visual C++ Developer On-line. This page has links to other C++ related sites and an article index. This site provides a free sample issue.

`http://www.vcdj.com/vcdj/default.asp`

Visit this site for professional articles and code examples. This site features columns containing book reviews, language integration and interviews.

`http://www.r2m.com/windev/`

This site is a great resource for windows development in C++. Links to code examples, programming tools and other C++ resources are provided.

`http://www.gamelan.com/`

This is one of the hottest sites for programmers. Gamelan offers links to C++, Java, ActiveX and VisualBasic. Code examples, tools, mailing lists, job opportunities and game development information are all provided at this site.

`http://www.activex.com/`

Cnet devotes this site to ActiveX. You can connect to the latest ActiveX news and information.

`http://www.active-x.com/`

The ActiveX Resource Center provides articles, VBScript samples and links to other ActiveX related sites.

`http://www.datamation.com/PlugIn/issues/1996/may15/`
    `DCOMDistributesObjectsButOnlyasfarasMicrosoft9.html`

This site is a developing resource for DCOM information.

`http://www.dbms.mfi.com/9611d14.html`

This is one of the most informative resources I found. It describes the relationship between DBMS, OLE, ActiveX and DCOM.

`http://www.neca.com/~vmis/durl.htm`

If you are looking for information on DCOM, this site provides an extensive list of relevant links.

`http://www.wcmh.com/lantimes/96may/605b001d.html`

LAN Times describes Microsoft's Distributed Component Object Model (DCOM) in an article titled "DCOM Could Ease OLE Apps Networking."

`http://www.microsoft.com/intdev/`

This Microsoft site has great information on ActiveX controls and links to ActiveX related sites.

`http://www.microsoft.com/intdev/controls/controls-f.htm`

Microsoft devotes this page to ActiveX controls. You can find a definition of ActiveX controls, examples from Microsoft and other companies, instructions on how to write your own controls and a list of FAQs.

Terminology

.dll file
ActiveX control
Add Tools dialog
Add Watch button in debugger
Application
Auto tab
binary-level specification
breakpoint
Breakpoints menu item
Breakpoints dialog
Build button
build
Build menu
Call Stack button in debugger
ClassView pane
Compile button
compiler
compiler error
compiler warning
Component Object Model (COM)
controls toolbar
Customize dialog
debugger
debugger toolbar
default project
dialog editor
disabled
Disassembly button in debugger

Dynamic Link Library (DLL)
editor
Execute menu item in **Build** menu
File menu
Files into Project menu item
FileView pane
focus
function
Functions list box
Functions Prototype list box
InfoView pane
Initial Directory field
Insert Files into Project dialog
Insert menu
Insert Resource dialog
Internet Explorer
ItypeLib dialog
left mouse button
Local tab
Microsoft Developer Studio
New dialog
New menu item of **File** menu
New Project Information dialog
New Project Workspace dialog
OCX control (**ActiveX** control)
Object Linking and Embedding (OLE)
OLE/COM Object Viewer menu item
OLE/COM Object Viewer dialog

Portability Tip

E.1   COM is language independent, compiler independent and location independent.

Testing and Debugging Tips

E.1   Microsoft Developer Studio's syntax color highlighting helps the programmer avoid using keywords accidentally as variable names.

E.2   If your program contains compiler errors, double click on an error message in the output window to point out the offending line of code. Visual C++ places a blue arrow next to the line of code in the source file.

E.3   Loops that iterate many times can be skipped by placing a breakpoint after the loop and clicking the **Go** button.

E.4   The debugger allows the user to "step into" C++ library functions.

E.5   Loops that iterate many times can be skipped by placing the cursor after the loop and clicking the **Run to Cursor** button.

E.6   Disabled breakpoints allow the programmer to maintain breakpoints in key locations in the program so they can be used again when they are needed. Disabled breakpoints are always visible.

E.7   When using the debugger, placing the mouse pointer over a variable name displays the variable's value.

E.8   When using the debugger to trace through a program, certain problems such as infinite loops can arise. These problems can usually be interrupted by selecting Break from the Debug menu.

Index

THE DEITEL SUITE OF PRODUCTS

BOOKS:

C++ How to Program, 2nd Edition

0-13-528910-6, 1998, 1200+pp Paper

The world's best-selling introductory C++ text, this book focuses on the principles of good software engineering with C++, and stresses program clarity and teaching by example. Revised and updated to cover the latest enhancements to the ANSI/ISO Draft Standard and the Standard Template Library, this second edition places a strong emphasis on pedagogy, with each concept of either C++ or object-oriented programming presented in the context of a complete, working C++ program followed by a screen capture showing the program's output. C++ How to Program, 2nd Edition includes a rich collection of exercises and valuable insight into common programming errors, as well as software engineering observations, portability tips, and debugging hints.

Java How to Program, 2nd Edition

0-13-899394-7, 1998, 1075pp Paper

In this revised 2nd edition, the Deitels introduce the fundamentals of object-oriented programming in Java. Every important aspect of Java is covered, updated for JDK 1.1, including the new graphical user interface features and delegation event handling model. Every program in the text has also been rewritten and recompiled to take advantage of the latest Java features. Among the learning devices are hundreds of "live code" programs with screen captures that show the outputs generated by that code, extensive exercises, many with answers, accompanying each chapter, and hundreds of tips, recommended practices, and cautions all marked with icons.

C How to Program, 2nd Edition

0-13-226119-7, 1994, 926 pp. Paper

Among the pedagogical devices featured in this best-selling introductory C text are a thorough use of the structured programming methodology, complete programs and sample outputs to demonstrate key C concepts, objectives and an outline at the beginning of every chapter, and a substantial collection of self-review exercises and answers. The result is a rigorous treatment of both theory and practice, including helpful sections on good programming practices, performance tips, and software engineering observations. The text also includes a 290-page introduction to C++.

visit us at: www.prenhall.com/deitel

... FROM PRENTICE HALL

BOOK/MULTIMEDIA PACKAGES:

 These complete book and interactive multimedia CD-ROM products are the perfect packages for anyone interested in learning Java or C++, and are exceptional and affordable resources for college students learning programming for the first time.

A Complete Java Training Course, 2nd Edition

0-13-790569-6, 1998, Boxed book and software

A Complete Java Training Course, 2nd Edition includes:

- The complete book *Java How to Program, 2nd Edition*
- A fully-interactive Multimedia Cyber Classroom CD-ROM that features:
  - 180+ complete Java programs with approximately 12,000 lines of working code;
  - Audio walkthroughs of key elements of the programs;
  - 1100+ questions and exercises over half of them with answers;
  - 400+ helpful hints and tips, marked with icons.

Built with Java, this product will run on the following Java-enabled platforms: Windows 95 and NT. Coming soon: versions for MacOS 8 and Solaris 2.5 and higher.

A Complete C++ Training Course, 2nd Edition

0-13-916305-0, 1998, Boxed book and software

A Complete C++ Training Course features:

- The complete, best-selling introductory book *C++ How to Program, 2nd Edition;*
- A fully-interactive Multimedia Cyber Classroom CD-ROM that features:
  — Hundreds of working programs that students can copy to a compiler;
  — Audio walkthroughs of key C++ concepts;
  — Hundreds of exercises, many complete with answers;
  — Thousands of hyperlinked index entries, with hypertext searching;
  — Helpful hints, marked with icons, that help teach good practices.

Built with Java, this product will run on the following Java-enabled platforms: Windows 95 and NT. Coming soon: versions for MacOS 8 and Solaries 2.5 and higher.

End-User License Agreement for Microsoft Software

MICROSOFT VISUAL C++, Learning Edition

IMPORTANT--READ CAREFULLY: This Microsoft End-User License Agreement ("EULA") is a legal agreement between you (either an individual or a single entity) and Microsoft Corporation for the Microsoft software product identified above, which includes computer software and may include associated media, printed materials, and "online" or electronic documentation ("SOFTWARE PRODUCT"). By installing, copying, or otherwise using the SOFTWARE PRODUCT, you agree to be bound by the terms of this EULA. If you do not agree to the terms of this EULA, do not install, copy, or use the SOFTWARE PRODUCT; you may; however, return it to your place of purchase for a full refund.

SOFTWARE PRODUCT LICENSE

The SOFTWARE PRODUCT is protected by copyright laws and international copyright treaties, as well as other intellectual property laws and treaties. The SOFTWARE PRODUCT is licensed, not sold.

1. **GRANT OF LICENSE.** This EULA grants you the following rights:

    a. **Software Product.** Microsoft grants to you as an individual, a personal, nonexclusive license to make and use copies of the SOFTWARE for the sole purposes of designing, developing, and testing software application(s). Except as provided in Section 2(a), you may install copies of the SOFTWARE PRODUCT on an unlimited number of computers provided that you are the only individual using the SOFTWARE PRODUCT in the manner provided above.

    b. **Electronic Documents.** Solely with respect to electronic documents included with the SOFTWARE PRODUCT, you may make an unlimited number of copies (either in hardcopy or electronic form), provided that such copies shall be used only for internal purposes and a re not republished or distributed to any third party,

    c. **Storage/Network Use.** You may also store or install a copy of the SOFTWARE PRODUCT on a storage device, such as a network server, used only to install or run the SOFTWARE PRODUCT on your computes over an internal network; however, you must acquire and dedicate a license for each separate computer on which the SOFTWARE PRODUCT is installed or run from a storage device. A license for the SOFTWARE PRODUCT may not be shared or used concurrently on different computers.

d. **Sample Code and Microsoft Foundation Classes.** In addition to the rights granted in Section 1(a), Microsoft grants you the right to use and modify the source code version of those portions of the SOFTWARE PRODUCT that are identified: (i) as the Microsoft Foundation Classes ("MFC"); and (ii) as sample code in the documentation and/or listed in the subdirectory Devstudio\VC\Samples located in the SOFTWARE PRODUCT (collectively, "SAMPLE CODE"), for the sole purposes of designing, developing, and testing your software applications(s), provided that you comply with Section 1(f), below.

e. **Redistributable Files.** *Provided* that you comply with Section 1(f), in addition to the rights granted in Section 1(a), Microsoft grants you a nonexclusive, royalty-free right to reproduce and distribute the object code version of the following portions of the SOFTWARE PRODUCT (collectively, the "REDISTRIBUTABLES"): (i) SAMPLE CODE (including any modifications you make): (ii) MFC (including any modifications you make); and (iii) the files identities in the Redistrb.wri file located in the SOFTWARE PRODUCT. For the purposes of this section, "modifications" shall mean enhancements to the functionality of the MPC or Sample Code.

f. **Redistribution Requirements.** If you redistribute the REDISTRIBUTABLES, you agree to (i) distribute the REDISTRIBUTABLES in object code only in conjunction with and as a part of a software application developed by you that adds significant and primary functionality to the REDISTRIBUTABLES and that is intended solely for noncommercial use of distribution ("Application"); (ii) not use Microsoft's name, logo, or trademarks to market your Application; (iii) include a valid copyright notice on your Application; (iv) indemnify, hold harmless, and defend Microsoft from and against any claims or lawsuits, including attorney's fees, that arise or result from the use or distribution of your Application; (v) not permit further distribution of the other terms of the REDISTRIBUTABLES by your end user. The following exception applies to Subsection (f)(v), above; provided that your end users comply with all the other terms of this EULA, you may permit your end users to reproduce and distribute the object code version of the files listed below ("COM Redistributables") only in conjunction with the redistribution of a Component Object Model (COM) object (e.g., an ActiveX control) designed or use or development of an Application and/or Web page that adds significant primary functionality to the COM Redistributables and that is intended for noncommercial use or distribution. COM Redistributables: Msvrt.dll, Mfc42.dll, Atl.dll, Msstkprp.dll, and Axdist.exe.

2. **DESCRIPTION OF OTHER RIGHTS AND LIMITATIONS.**

a. **Academic Edition Software.** If the SOFTWARE PRODUCT is identified as "Academic Edition" or "AE," you must be a "Qualified Educational User" to use the SOFTWARE PRODUCT. To determine whether you rae a Qualified Educational User, please contact Microsoft Sales Information Center/One Microsoft Way/Redmond, WA 98052-6399 or the Microsoft subsidiary serving your country,

b. **Not for Resale Software.** If the SOFTWARE PRODUCT is labeled "Not of Resale" or "NFR," then notwithstanding other sections of this EULA, you may not resell, or otherwise transfer for value, the SOFTWARE PRODUCT.

c.   **Limitations on Reverse Engineering, Decompilation, and Disassembly.** You may not reverse engineer, decompile, or disassemble the SOFTWARE PRODUCT, except and only to the extent that such activity is expressly permitted by applicable law not-withstanding this limitation.

d.   **No Separation of Components.** The SOFTWARE PRODUCT is licensed as a single product and neither the software programs making up the SOFTWARE PRODUCT nor any UPDATE may be separated for use by more than one user at a time.

e.   **Rental.** You may not rent or lease the SOFTWARE PRODUCT.

f.   Support Services. Microsoft may provide you with support services related to the SOFTWARE PRODUCT ("Support Services"). Use of SUpport Services is governed by the Microsoft policies and programs described in the user manual, "online" docu-mentation and/or other Microsoft-provided materials. Any supplemental software code provided to you as part of the Support Services shall be considered part of the SOFT-WARE PRODUCT and subject to the terms and conditions of this EULA,. With respect to technical information you provide to Microsoft as part of the Support ser-vices, Microsoft may use such information for its business purposes, including for product support and development. Microsoft will not utilize such technical information in a form that personally identifies you.

g.   **Software Transfer.** You may permanently transfer all of your rights under this EULA, provided that you retain no copies, you transfer all of the SOFTWARE PRODUCT (including all component parts, the media and printed materials, any upgrades, this EULA, and, if applicable, the Certificate of Authenticity), and the recipient agrees to the terms of this EULA. If the SOFTWARE PRODUCT is an upgrade, any transfer must include all prior versions of the SOFTWARE PRODUCT.

h.   **Termination.** Without prejudice to any other rights, Microsoft may terminate this EULA if you fail to comply with the terms and conditions of this EULA. In such event, you must destroy all copies of the SOFTWARE PRODUCT. In addition, your rights under this EULA that pertain to the Microsoft Internet Explorer software shall termi-nate upon termination of your Microsoft operating system product EULA

3.   **UPGRADES.** If the SOFTWARE is labeled as an upgrade, you must be properly licensed to use a product identified by Microsoft as being eligible for upgrade in order use the SOFT-WARE PRODUCT. A SOFTWARE PRODUCT labeled as an upgrade replaces and/or supple-ments the product that formed the basis for your eligibility for the upgrade. You may use the resulting upgraded product only in accordance with the terms of this EULA. If the SOFT-WARE PRODUCT is an upgrade of a component of a package of software programs that you licensed as a single product the SOFTWARE PRODUCT may be used and transferred only as part of that product package and may not be separated for use on more than one computer.

4.   **COPYRIGHT.** All title and copyrights in and to the SOFTWARE PRODUCT (including but not limited to any images, photographs, animations, video, audio, music, text, and "applets" incorporated into the SOFTWARE PRODUCT), the accompanying printed materials, and any copies of the SOFTWARE PRODUCT are owned by Microsoft or its suppliers. The SOFT-WARE PRODUCT is protected by copyright laws and international treaty provisions. There-fore, you must treat the SOFTWARE PRODUCT like any other copyrighted material except that you may install the SOFTWARE PRODUCT on a single computer provided you keep the original solely for backup or archival purposes. You may not copy the printed materials accompanying the SOFTWARE PRODUCT.

5. **DUAL MEDIA SOFTWARE.** You may receive the SOFTWARE PRODUCT in more than one medium. Regardless of the type or size of medium you receive, you may use only one medium that is appropriate for your single computer. You may not use or install the SOFTWARE PRODUCT on a single computer provided you keep the original solely for backup or archival purposes. You may not copy the printed materials accompanying the SOFTWARE PRODUCT.

6. **U.S. GOVERNMENT RESTRICTED RIGHTS.** The SOFTWARE PRODUCT and documentation are provided with RESTRICTED RIGHTS. Use, duplication, or disclosure by the Government is subject to restrictions as set forth in subparagraph (c)(1)(ii) of the Rights in Technical Data and Computer Software clause at DFARS 252.227-7013 or subparagraphs (c)(1) and (2) of the Commercial Computer Software-Restricted Rights at 48 CFR 52.227-19, as applicable. Manufacturer is Microsoft Corporation/One Microsoft Way/Redmond, WA 98052-6399.

7. **EXPORT RESTRICTIONS.** You agree that you will not export or re-export the SOFTWARE PRODUCT to any country, person, entity or end user subject to U.S.A. export restrictions. Restricted countries currently include, but are not necessarily limited to Cuba, Iran, Iraq, Libya, North Korea, Syria, and the Federal Republic of Yugoslavia (Serbia and Montenegro, U.N. Protected Areas and areas of Republic of Bosnia and Herzegovina under the control of Bosnian Serb forces). You warrant and represent that neither the U.S.A. Bureau of Export Administration nor any other federal agency has suspended, revoked or denied your export privileges.

MISCELLANEOUS

If you acquired this product in the United States, this EULA is governed by the laws of the State of Washington.

If you acquired this product in Canada, this EULA is governed by the laws of the Province of Ontario, Canada. Each of the parties hereto irrevocably attorns to the jurisdiction of the courts of the Province of Ontario and further agrees to commence any litigation which may arise hereunder in the courts located in the Judicial District of York, Province of Ontario.

If this product was acquired outside the United States, then local law may apply.

Should you have any questions concerning this EULA, or if you desire to contact Microsoft for any reason, please contact the Microsoft subsidiary serving your country, or write: Microsoft Sales Information Center/One Microsoft Way/Redmond, WA 98052-6399.

LIMITED WARRANTY

NO WARRANTIES. Microsoft expressly disclaims any warranty for the SOFTWARE PRODUCT. The SOFTWARE PRODUCT and any related documentation is provided "as is" without warranty of any kind, either express or implied, including, without limitation, the implied warranties or merchantability, fitness for a particular purpose, or noninfringement. The entire risk arising out of use or performance of the SOFTWARE PRODUCT remains with you.

NO LIABILITY FOR CONSEQUENTIAL DAMAGES. In no event shall Microsoft or its suppliers be liable for any damages whatsoever (including, without limitation, damages fro loss of business profits, business interruption, loss of business information, or any other pecuniary loss) arising out of the use of or inability to use this Microsoft product, even if Microsoft has been advised of the possibility of such damages. Because some states/jurisdictions do not allow the exclusion or limitation of liability for consequential or incidental damages, the above limitation may not apply to you.

The program on the enclosed CD-ROM was reproduced by Prentice Hall under a special agreement with Microsoft Corporation. For this reason, Prentice Hall is responsible for the product warranty and for support. If your disk is defective, return it to Prentice Hall, which will arrange for its replacement. Any product support will be provided, if at all, by Prentice Hall. PLEASE DO NOT CONTACT MIRCROSOFT CORPORATION FOR PRODUCT SUPPORT. End users of the Microsoft program shall not be considered "registered owners" of a Microsoft product and therefore shall not be eligible for upgrades, promotions or other benefits available to "registered owners" of Microsoft products.

LICENSE AGREEMENT AND LIMITED WARRANTY

READ THE FOLLOWING TERMS AND CONDITIONS CAREFULLY BEFORE OPENING THIS SOFTWARE PACKAGE. THIS LEGAL DOCUMENT IS AN AGREEMENT BETWEEN YOU AND PRENTICE-HALL, INC. (THE "COMPANY"). BY OPENING THIS SEALED SOFTWARE PACKAGE, YOU ARE AGREEING TO BE BOUND BY THESE TERMS AND CONDITIONS. IF YOU DO NOT AGREE WITH THESE TERMS AND CONDITIONS, DO NOT OPEN THE SOFTWARE PACKAGE. PROMPTLY RETURN THE UNOPENED SOFTWARE PACKAGE AND ALL ACCOMPANYING ITEMS TO THE PLACE YOU OBTAINED THEM FOR A FULL REFUND OF ANY SUMS YOU HAVE PAID.

1.　　　GRANT OF LICENSE: In consideration of your purchase of this book, and your agreement to abide by the terms and conditions of this Agreement, the Company grants to you a nonexclusive right to use and display the copy of the enclosed software program (hereinafter the "SOFTWARE") on a single computer (i.e., with a single CPU) at a single location so long as you comply with the terms of this Agreement. The Company reserves all rights not expressly granted to you under this Agreement.

2.　　　OWNERSHIP OF SOFTWARE: You own only the magnetic or physical media (the enclosed media) on which the SOFTWARE is recorded or fixed, but the Company and the software developers retain all the rights, title, and ownership to the SOFTWARE recorded on the original media copy(ies) and all subsequent copies of the SOFTWARE, regardless of the form or media on which the original or other copies may exist. This license is not a sale of the original SOFTWARE or any copy to you.

3.　　　COPY RESTRICTIONS: This SOFTWARE and the accompanying printed materials and user manual (the "Documentation") are the subject of copyright. The individual programs on the media are copyrighted by the authors of each program. Some of the programs on the media include separate licensing agreements. If you intend to use one of these programs, you must read and follow its accompanying license agreement. You may not copy the Documentation or the SOFTWARE, except that you may make a single copy of the SOFTWARE for backup or archival purposes only. You may be held legally responsible for any copying or copyright infringement which is caused or encouraged by your failure to abide by the terms of this restriction.

4.　　　USE RESTRICTIONS: You may not network the SOFTWARE or otherwise use it on more than one computer or computer terminal at the same time. You may physically transfer the SOFTWARE from one computer to another provided that the SOFTWARE is used on only one computer at a time. You may not distribute copies of the SOFTWARE or Documentation to others. You may not reverse engineer, disassemble, decompile, modify, adapt, translate, or create derivative works based on the SOFTWARE or the Documentation without the prior written consent of the Company.

5.　　　TRANSFER RESTRICTIONS: The enclosed SOFTWARE is licensed only to you and may not be transferred to any one else without the prior written consent of the Company. Any unauthorized transfer of the SOFTWARE shall result in the immediate termination of this Agreement.

6.　　　TERMINATION: This license is effective until terminated. This license will terminate automatically without notice from the Company and become null and void if you fail to comply with any provisions or limitations of this license. Upon termination, you shall destroy the Documentation and all copies of the SOFTWARE. All provisions of this Agreement as to warranties, limitation of liability, remedies or damages, and our ownership rights shall survive termination.

7.   MISCELLANEOUS: This Agreement shall be construed in accordance with the laws of the United States of America and the State of New York and shall benefit the Company, its affiliates, and assignees.

8.   LIMITED WARRANTY AND DISCLAIMER OF WARRANTY: The Company warrants that the SOFTWARE, when properly used in accordance with the Documentation, will operate in substantial conformity with the description of the SOFTWARE set forth in the Documentation. The Company does not warrant that the SOFTWARE will meet your requirements or that the operation of the SOFTWARE will be uninterrupted or error-free. The Company warrants that the media on which the SOFTWARE is delivered shall be free from defects in materials and workmanship under normal use for a period of thirty (30) days from the date of your purchase. Your only remedy and the Company's only obligation under these limited warranties is, at the Company's option, return of the warranted item for a refund of any amounts paid by you or replacement of the item. Any replacement of SOFTWARE or media under the warranties shall not extend the original warranty period. The limited warranty set forth above shall not apply to any SOFTWARE which the Company determines in good faith has been subject to misuse, neglect, improper installation, repair, alteration, or damage by you. EXCEPT FOR THE EXPRESSED WARRANTIES SET FORTH ABOVE, THE COMPANY DISCLAIMS ALL WARRANTIES, EXPRESS OR IMPLIED, INCLUDING WITHOUT LIMITATION, THE IMPLIED WARRANTIES OF MERCHANTABILITY AND FITNESS FOR A PARTICULAR PURPOSE. EXCEPT FOR THE EXPRESS WARRANTY SET FORTH ABOVE, THE COMPANY DOES NOT WARRANT, GUARANTEE, OR MAKE ANY REPRESENTATION REGARDING THE USE OR THE RESULTS OF THE USE OF THE SOFTWARE IN TERMS OF ITS CORRECTNESS, ACCURACY, RELIABILITY, CURRENTNESS, OR OTHERWISE.

IN NO EVENT, SHALL THE COMPANY OR ITS EMPLOYEES, AGENTS, SUPPLIERS, OR CONTRACTORS BE LIABLE FOR ANY INCIDENTAL, INDIRECT, SPECIAL, OR CONSEQUENTIAL DAMAGES ARISING OUT OF OR IN CONNECTION WITH THE LICENSE GRANTED UNDER THIS AGREEMENT, OR FOR LOSS OF USE, LOSS OF DATA, LOSS OF INCOME OR PROFIT, OR OTHER LOSSES, SUSTAINED AS A RESULT OF INJURY TO ANY PERSON, OR LOSS OF OR DAMAGE TO PROPERTY, OR CLAIMS OF THIRD PARTIES, EVEN IF THE COMPANY OR AN AUTHORIZED REPRESENTATIVE OF THE COMPANY HAS BEEN ADVISED OF THE POSSIBILITY OF SUCH DAMAGES. IN NO EVENT SHALL LIABILITY OF THE COMPANY FOR DAMAGES WITH RESPECT TO THE SOFTWARE EXCEED THE AMOUNTS ACTUALLY PAID BY YOU, IF ANY, FOR THE SOFTWARE.

SOME JURISDICTIONS DO NOT ALLOW THE LIMITATION OF IMPLIED WARRANTIES OR LIABILITY FOR INCIDENTAL, INDIRECT,

SPECIAL, OR CONSEQUENTIAL DAMAGES, SO THE ABOVE LIMITATIONS MAY NOT ALWAYS APPLY. THE WARRANTIES IN THIS AGREEMENT GIVE YOU SPECIFIC LEGAL RIGHTS AND YOU MAY ALSO HAVE OTHER RIGHTS WHICH VARY IN ACCORDANCE WITH LOCAL LAW.
ACKNOWLEDGMENT

YOU ACKNOWLEDGE THAT YOU HAVE READ THIS AGREEMENT, UNDERSTAND IT, AND AGREE TO BE BOUND BY ITS TERMS AND CONDITIONS. YOU ALSO AGREE THAT THIS AGREEMENT IS THE COMPLETE AND EXCLUSIVE STATEMENT OF THE AGREEMENT BETWEEN YOU AND THE COMPANY AND SUPERSEDES ALL PROPOSALS OR PRIOR AGREEMENTS, ORAL, OR WRITTEN, AND ANY OTHER COMMUNICATIONS BETWEEN YOU AND THE COMPANY OR ANY REPRESENTATIVE OF THE COMPANY RELATING TO THE SUBJECT MATTER OF THIS AGREEMENT.

Should you have any questions concerning this Agreement or if you wish to contact the Company for any reason, please contact in writing at the address below.

Robin Short
Prentice Hall PTR
One Lake Street
Upper Saddle River, New Jersey 07458

LICENSE AGREEMENT
AND LIMITED WARRANTY

SYSTEM REQUIREMENTS

To run Visual C++, Learning Edition, you need:

- *PC with a 486DX/66 MHz or higher processor (Pentium 90 recommended)*
- *Microsoft Windows 95 operating system or WIndows NT® Workstation operating system version 4.0 or later*
- *20 MB of RAM (24 MB recommended)*
- *Hard-disk space required:*
  - *Typical installation: 175 MB*
  - *Minimum installation: 120MB*
  - *CD-ROM installation: (tools run from the compact disc): 50 MB*
  - *Total tools and information on the disc: 650MB*
- *CD-ROM drive*
- *32-bit protected mode CD-ROM driver*
- *VGA or higher-resolution monitor (Super VGA recommended)*
- *Microsoft Mouse or compatible pointing device*

CD KEY:
636-6824537

Don't Lose This Number!
You must use it every time you install this software.
